A U S T R A L I A

BENEATH THE SOUTHERN CROSS

Text and
Photography by
SUE and BRIAN KENDRICK

A Lightstorm Publication

F O R E W O R D

There are many coffee table books on Australia so one could ask why another? This is however no ordinary picture book. It is a visual diary of a remarkable 55,000 kilometre journey undertaken by a young photographer, her husband and following his birth *en route*, their baby son. Sue Kendrick qualified as a photographer over ten years ago, but together with her husband Brian gave up a thriving practice in Sydney to live under the stars and photograph our wild and wonderful landscape - our Australia.

In their photographs the Australian landscape seems at times evocative of other scenes: the outback reminiscent of South American pampas, the red desert interior like the great national parks of Arizona, whilst the sugar cane plantations of Queensland could be in the West Indies. On closer examination these images are uniquely Australian; the interiors of outback pubs, the ghost gums, the vivid colours of the Pinnacles against a deep blue southern sky, the Aborigines and their art. As Sue and Brian explore the myths and legends of this vast land the photographs reveal that intimate and delicate balance between man and his environment. What other place on earth could present such varied and interesting images? There are few places left in the world that possess such purity in the quality of light. From the dawn on Lake St. Clair through the harsh morning light on balancing rock to the late afternoon at Point Quobba and the sunset at Rainbow Valley, Sue and Brian have successfully captured that unique quality for us all to enjoy.

The photographers' eye for detail reveals yet other aspects unseen by the casual observer; the log in the dew, the water lily, the colour changes of an alpine gum, the shell in the sand. Like anyone's vision of our land Sue and Brian's is an intensely personal record - theirs reflects the relationship between the early settlers of this huge continent and the land itself - but theirs is made accessible to all through the publication of this wonderful book. Now we can all evoke those times long past and enjoy those delicate dawns and sumptuous sunsets seen only by those who camp in the outback - indeed seen only by those who sleep 'beneath the Southern Cross.'

A.R Williams

Dr Robin Williams PhD DGPh FRPS FBIPP FIMI FRMS FISTC FBPA
Professor of Photography & Head of Department of Visual Communication
Royal Melbourne Institute of Technology

This book is dedicated to Barbara and Hugh.
Not only did they travel to the far reaches of the continent to visit their grandson, but their unfailing support and encouragement were always appreciated.

A C K N O W L E D G E M E N T S

We sincerely thank the following organisations for their support

Bond Colour Laboratories
4 Gwynne Street
Richmond Vic 3121
Ph: (03) 429 1299

For digitally combining two transparencies to create the striking image on the cover.

Hanimex Pty Ltd
108 Old Pittwater Rd,
Brookvale NSW 2100
Ph: (02) 938 0400

For providing the marvellous Velvia and Fujichrome 100D film, which faithfully recorded the vivid colours and subtle hues of the Australian landscape.

L&P Photographic Supplies
96 Reserve Rd, Artarmon NSW 2064
Ph: (02) 906 2733
95 Rundle St, Kent Town SA 5067
Ph: (08) 363 1783

For supply and service of photographic equipment and unparalleled technical expertise.

Many of the images reproduced in this book are available as limited edition photographic prints and/or posters. For more information see pages 178/179.

A Lightstorm Photography Production
Published by Lightstorm Publishing
P.O. Box 1167, Nowra NSW 2541
Ph: (044) 46 6007 Fax: (044) 46 6008

First Published 1994
© Copyright: Photographs and text
Sue & Brian Kendrick 1994
Designed by Anne Esposito
Printed by Dai Nippon

National Library of Australia
Cataloguing-in-Publication data

Kendrick, Sue.
   Australia beneath the Southern Cross.

   Includes index.
   ISBN 0 646 17671 4.

   1. Australia - Pictorial works. 2. Australia - History.
   3. Australia - Description and travel. I. Kendrick, Brian.
   II. Title.

994

Cover:	The brilliant stars scribe their arc through the evening sky above the glowing mass of Uluru.
Endpapers:	An approaching storm casts its blue shadow over the Twelve Apostles, Port Campbell National Park, Victoria.
Page 1:	Dawn at the Pink Roadhouse, Oodnadatta, South Australia.
Page 2:	The glowing cliffs surrounding Edith Falls, Nitmiluk National Park, Northern Territory.
Pages 4-5:	The still waters of O'Shannassy Creek, western Queensland.
Pages 6-7:	Brick red termite mounds on Morstone Station, western Queensland.
Pages 8-9:	Mosses colonise a fallen log at Central Station on Fraser Island, Queensland.
Page 11:	A wind sculptured dune of the Strzelecki Desert, South Australia.
Pages 12-13:	A lily covered billabong in Lakefield National Park, Cape York, Queensland.
Rear Cover:	Stone hut on Cordillo Downs Station, South Australia.

CONTENTS

INTRODUCTION

Like many Australians we had a dream to travel Australia, to spend some time in the remote and rugged parts of the continent where legends had been born. In March 1992 we realised our dream when, with our business sold, worldly goods in storage and farewells said, we were finally ready to 'hit the wallaby'.

Having lived in cities all our lives, leaving the big smoke behind wasn't quite as simple as driving south and onto the open road. All the stresses and strains of selling a business, packing up the house and preparing for our journey took some time to dissipate. But, like the snake that has shed its old skin and is no longer restricted by external forces, we soon began to enjoy our new-found freedom to move as and when the fancy took us.

Our plan was to travel to the less populated regions of the continent; to avoid the cities and towns as much as possible and to feel the solitude of the vast, empty spaces of this huge land. We wanted to explore and photograph the places where the legends began, travel in the footsteps of the pioneers, hear the Dreamtime stories of the Aboriginal people and meet those who still live in isolation. Today's legends drew us as well; we wanted to travel the infamous Gibb River Road, explore the Bungle Bungles, visit the wetlands of Kakadu and fish for tailor on Fraser Island. We wanted to meet the legendary Molly Clark of Old Andado Station, have a cuppa at Cameron's Corner and eat 'Beef and Barra' at the Daly Waters pub.

With Sydney as our starting point we travelled in a rough figure eight around the continent. Our son Stewart, born after three months of travel, experienced the journey with us. We hiked into Mitchell Falls, climbed Ayers Rock, fished for barramundi in the Kimberley, soaked in the thermal springs at Mataranka and had a beer (or two) in the Birdsville pub. Together, we experienced the changing moods of the landscape, the vastness of the interior and the awesome power of the oceans. We were savaged by mosquitoes, plagued by flies, raided by mice, dehydrated by the searing desert sun and frozen by the southern gales. We enjoyed the solitude of the desert sunset, the mist on the water at dawn, the sight of sea eagles catching fish and the companionship of the people we met. We felt the spirit of those who'd gone before us as we read the stories of their foolhardy adventures, their courage in the face of adversity, their successes and failures.

We camped in the bush, by dry creek beds, on cattle and sheep stations, in campgrounds, on the beach and in friends' backyards; we stayed in the lighthouse keeper's cottage on Kangaroo Island and in country pubs from time to time. We slept to the sounds of the bush, the faraway beat of the pub juke box or the distant throb of a station generator, but wherever we were the Southern Cross shone above us like our personal lucky charm, as it had shone on all those who'd travelled before us.

All Australians have an association with the Southern Cross; it appears on our flag, in Aboriginal Dreamtime stories and throughout Australian literature from the earliest writings. Early navigators used this constellation to establish the position of the South Celestial Pole, and it was in a plane named the *Southern Cross* that Charles Kingsford-Smith and C.T.P. Ulm made the first air crossing of the Pacific in 1928. Whatever your association with this unique constellation, we trust you will enjoy your travels as you join us on our journey of discovery 'Beneath the Southern Cross'.

SOUTHERN EXPOSURE

▶ When you're asked to think of images that typify Australia, it's visions of the outback which spring readily to mind. Of rolling red sand dunes, ghost gums, windmills and stockmen silhouetted against the sunset; of slab huts with corrugated iron roofs and long-legged kids playing in the dust; of station women in Akubras squinting into the sun and men drinking beer on pub verandahs. Yet Australia is fringed with 22,000 kilometres of magnificent coastline and most of the population live on a narrow strip of land on the eastern seaboard, between the temperate waters of the Pacific and the Great Dividing Range. In the early days of Australia's European settlement, while a few bold explorers were being drawn into the dry and dusty interior in search of an inland sea, most of the drama was being played out around the coast.

▶ In search of some early maritime legends, our journey took us rapidly south and into the treacherous waters of Bass Strait. The strait is a narrow, shallow passage of water which separates Tasmania from the mainland, but that was not always the case. As recently as the last ice age, the islands of the Furneaux Group, in the east of the strait, formed a land bridge to the mainland. When the sea level rose at the end of the ice age, Tasmania was left stranded and the islands of the Furneaux Group were surrounded by shoals and dangerous reefs. As you experience the tranquillity of these islands today, it's difficult to imagine their reckless and bloody past. But these wild waters attracted wild men, seeking their fortune from the skins of seals and the blubber of whales, which were once prolific in this region. The sealers and whalers abducted Aboriginal women as 'wives', and plundering was commonplace. It wasn't until the seals and whales were hunted to near-extinction that the islands experienced a kind of peace once again. Some of the Aboriginal women who'd been abducted by the sealers stayed on and many of the islanders today are their direct descendants.

▶ By the early years of this century, fishing and cattle farming, along with the traditional Aboriginal industry of mutton-birding, had replaced the brutal industries of the past. Yet for decades the islanders remained incredibly isolated, relying on small coastal cutters to ferry stock, passengers and provisions between the islands and the mainland. The cutters were captained by brave men, who navigated the ever-changing shoals of the strait, often in fearsome storms. Many lost their lives, but the bravery of them all was typified by George 'Mac' McCarthy, when his boat the *Willwatch* finally went down in 1959. After struggling for many hours in heavy seas, his ship taking water and bilge pumps inoperative, he lost the battle to bring his old vessel under control. As he ordered his crew to abandon ship, his last words on the radio were, 'It looks as if this is it...see you later...cheerio.' The strait had claimed another victim.

▶ One of Australia's best known maritime tragedies happened long before the *Willwatch* went down. Not very many nautical miles away, on what became known as Victoria's 'Shipwreck Coast', more than 60 vessels were claimed by the sea last century. Of these, none were more tragic than the loss of the iron sailing ship, the *Loch Ard*, which was carrying passengers and cargo from London to Melbourne. The ship was less than a day's sail from her destination when disaster struck. In the early hours of June 1st, 1878, the crew suddenly noticed white water and before the ship could be brought about she ran aground on a reef off the Port Campbell coastline. Fifty-two of the 54 people aboard lost their lives in the pounding surf on that June morning. A ship's apprentice named Tom Pearce and a passenger, Eva Carmichael, who managed to get ashore at what is now known as the Loch Ard Gorge, were the only survivors. In the days that followed only five bodies were recovered from the sea, Eva Carmichael's mother and one of her sisters among them. The bodies of her father, two brothers and two other sisters were never found. Tom Pearce was later awarded a medal for his bravery

in saving Eva, then scaling the cliffs to search for help. The press stirred people's imaginations and there were many who hoped the two might marry, but Eva later returned to England and, though they corresponded briefly, they never met again.

▶ The small amount of cargo which was eventually salvaged from the wreck of the *Loch Ard* included a magnificent porcelain peacock, 1.5 metres in height, which was destined for the Melbourne Exhibition of 1880. Amazingly, it suffered only a small chip to its beak during the ordeal. Almost 100 years later, the bird was purchased for display at the Flagstaff Hill Maritime Village Museum in nearby Warnambool. Even today, shards of broken china from the wreck may well be found among the shifting sands of the shoreline in the Loch Ard Gorge. The clifftop cemetery overlooking the site is an evocative reminder of the tragedy.

▶ Tragedy also played its part in the early days of European settlement on Kangaroo Island, some 500 kilometres to the west. In the early days it had the reputation of being one of the three 'islands of wrecks', along with King Island in Bass Strait and Fraser Island off the Queensland coast.

▶ Fifty vessels were to founder in the waters surrounding Kangaroo Island before the completion of three lighthouses - Cape Willoughby in 1852, Cape Borda in 1858 and Cape Du Couedic in 1909. With a supply ship calling only four times a year, it was a remote existence for the lighthouse keepers and their families. Perched atop the high cliffs of Kangaroo Island's north-west coast, the Cape Borda Light was maintained by three lighthouse keepers, working in shifts around the clock. When the supply ship made its three-monthly visit, provisions had to be rowed ashore, landed on a beach below the lighthouse, then hauled up the cliff face. This extreme isolation and lack of contact with the outside world ended in tragedy for the first head keeper, Captain Woodward. The light had been operative for barely two months when he tripped and fell on a stick which pierced his eye. With no passing ships to render assistance, he died three weeks later from a resulting infection.

▶ Like the islands of Bass Strait, Kangaroo Island's prolific wildlife attracted whalers, sealers and fur trappers in the early years of the nineteenth century. Although 'discovered' by Flinders in 1802, the island wasn't officially inhabited by the British until 1836. In the meantime, a murderous group of escaped convicts and ship's deserters settled there. Dressed in skins, they bartered salt and animal pelts with the passing whaling ships for rum, tea, flour and sugar. They, too, kidnapped Aboriginal women from Tasmania and the mainland and took them as 'wives'. One of these ruffians was George 'Fireball' Bates, a deserter of the Royal Navy, who was so-named because of his flaming red hair and whiskers. This infamous character led violent raids to the mainland and abducted women of the Narinyerri tribe. To escape this murderous villain, it is said that one of the women swam the 14 kilometres back to the mainland with her baby strapped to her back!

▶ Eventually Britain, having long feared that the French and others may have had designs on Australia's southern coastline, set about cleaning up Kangaroo Island in preparation for colonisation. Many of the renegades who'd inhabited the island were taken back to Port Jackson in chains, leaving only a handful of islanders behind.

▶ Due to its lack of fresh water, it wasn't Kangaroo Island but Adelaide which was chosen as the location for the first British settlement in South Australia. There, Colonel Light planned a city surrounded by parks and gardens and the beauty of Adelaide today owes much to his vision. Today, Kangaroo Island is a popular tourist destination, with its resident seal colonies, tame kangaroos, flocks of Cape Barren geese and wild scenic beauty.

Right: This cascade on Conglomerate Creek, in the Victorian high country, can be reached by a walk which takes you past Guy's Hut, a typical cattlemen's shelter of timber slabs and corrugated iron. The creek flows through alpine meadows before it plummets 30 metres into Bryce's Gorge.

Previous page: A sudden mist rolls in to wet the multi-coloured bark of this snow gum in the high country of Victoria. Even in late summer, when the alpine flowers are blooming, the temperature can drop to below freezing and snow falls are not uncommon.

At Lake Dobson, in Tasmania's Mount Field National Park, a snow gum hugs the water's edge. A short walk around the perimeter of the lake leads through groves of pandanus palms and giant paperbarks. Declared as a National Park in 1916, Mount Field is one of Tasmania's oldest and most popular natural regions.

Early morning mist lifts from the waters of Lake Dobson to reveal a beautiful autumn day. In winter, snow attracts cross country skiers to the park, while in the summer months bushwalkers flock to the area to enjoy spectacular scenery and alpine flowers.

Left: Like spidery fingers, the twigs of a submerged branch pierce the still waters of Lake Dobson in Tasmania's Mount Field National Park.

Right: Not very far away, a gentle walk through lush rainforest leads to Russell Falls, which cascade like a veil over glistening black mudstone.

The sun's rays refract the airborne spray into a delicate rainbow at the base of Montezuma Falls, situated between the towns of Rosebery and Zeehan in Tasmania's west. The falls are reached by a delightful 8-kilometre walk through rainforest, following the disused railway of a now defunct tin mine. You hear the deafening roar of the falls long before you see them plunging 113 metres to the rocks below.

One of the rustic old rail bridges which led from the tin mine to the smelter. Tin was discovered in the region in 1879, sparking a rush to the west coast. Later discoveries of copper and silver-lead boosted the population of Zeehan to 10,000 by the turn of the century. At that time the town was serviced by 26 hotels and boasted Australia's largest theatre, the Gaiety, where Dame Nellie Melba sang. Although tourism is of increasing importance, mining remains a significant industry.

A lovely old boat shed stands on the shores of Lake Dove, in Tasmania's Cradle Mountain-Lake St Clair National Park. Nearby is the commencement of the 85-kilometre Overland Track, which traverses the park. Taking five to ten days to complete, the walk leads through ancient myrtle forests, groves of pandanus palms and across alpine moors carpeted with wildflowers.

Right: Generally shrouded in cloud, a clear autumn day reveals the imposing ramparts of Cradle Mountain. When Austrian born pioneer of the region Gustav Weindorfer first stood atop Cradle Mountain he declared, "This must be a National Park for all time." Due to his vision and that of others who followed him, the park is now inscribed on the UNESCO World Heritage List.

Eighty-five kilometres away, at the other end of the Overland Track, lie the tranquil waters of Lake St Clair. With a depth of more than 200 metres, the lake occupies a basin gouged by two glaciers about 15,000 years ago. The park is famous for its bushwalking, trout fishing and wildlife, which includes spotted quolls and Tasmanian devils.

In the sleepy fishing village of Bridport, on Tasmania's north coast, the late afternoon sun caresses the new paintwork of an old boat.

Overleaf: The distant view is blurred by the misty rain of an approaching storm.

Coloured by the setting sun, a small boat is left marooned by the receding tide.

In the calm of dawn an old warehouse on Flinders Island reflects the pinkish tints of the coming day. Situated in Bass Strait, Flinders Island is one of the Furneaux Group and at various times in geological history has been part of a land bridge linking Tasmania with the mainland. Each spring, millions of mutton birds return to these islands to nest. The harvesting of mutton bird chicks for food, oil, down and by-products has been practised since Aboriginal times and still remains an important industry on the islands of Bass Strait.

While the mountains of the Freycinet Peninsula stand brooding in the background the setting sun illuminates the rocky shoreline. This region was declared as Freycinet National Park in 1916, having been recognised as an important wilderness area. Today it is a popular destination for travellers, attracted by its tame wildlife, magnificent wildflowers and many walking paths.

Nature's paintbrush has decorated the cliffs of Maria Island in earthy tones. The tranquillity of this island, located off Tasmania's east coast, belies its varied and sometimes bloody past, including two separate eras of convict settlement. There followed a period of wine and silk production before sheep and cattle farming replaced the vines. These days Maria Island is an important wildlife sanctuary which is home to more than 130 species of birds including the rare forty-spotted pardalote.

The eerie light of an approaching storm casts its blue shadow over the Twelve Apostles. Among Victoria's most famous landmarks, the Apostles are located on the 'Shipwreck Coast', a rugged and notorious coastline which claimed more than 60 vessels last century. The most famous wreck of these treacherous waters was the iron sailing ship, the *Loch Ard,* which ran aground in thick fog in the early hours of June 1st, 1878. Of the 54 passengers and crew, only two survived the disaster.

The setting sun reflects warmly from the cliffs of the Port Campbell National Park, which encompasses the Twelve Apostles. Years of undercutting of the soft limestone have resulted in remnant stacks which stand proudly amidst the swirling surf.

On a summer's evening in 1990 the landward arch of London Bridge, in Port Campbell National Park, collapsed into the sea leaving two tourists stranded. Lucky to escape with their lives, they were rescued by helicopter some hours later. The constant onslaught of the elements had gradually eroded the base of the arch, leading to the collapse.

The jagged rocks of Admirals Arch frame the treacherous waters of Cape Du Couedic on Kangaroo Island, off the coast of South Australia. The island was 'discovered' by the British navigator Matthew Flinders in 1802 and was a welcome sight for the crew. Having been denied fresh provisions after many months at sea, they took advantage of the prolific wildlife, slaughtering many kangaroos and other animals for fresh meat. It was Flinders who bestowed the name Kangaroo Island.

Glowing in the setting sun, the sheltered waters of Stokes Bay on Kangaroo Island are popular for swimming.
A natural tunnel through limestone boulders leads to this secluded beach.

Silhouetted by the rising sun, the Remarkable Rocks overlook Kangaroo Island's southern coastline. Situated in Flinders Chase National Park, this section of coast is home to both sea lions and fur seals. Hunted to the brink of extinction in the early years of the nineteenth century, both species are now protected in a series of parks and reserves including Flinders Chase, Seal Bay, Cape Gantheaume, Kelly Hill and Vivonne Bay.

The Remarkable Rocks lie scattered atop a massive granite dome, with the waters of the Southern Ocean pounding the cliffs below. Salt spray and strong winds have eroded the rocks to form the remarkable shapes we see today, while encrusting lichens tint their surface in orange and pink tones.

Left: The lighthouse at Cape Du Couedic flashes its message of warning to passing boats. Over 50 vessels came to grief on Kangaroo Island's rugged shores before three lighthouses were built to warn others of the danger. Cape Du Couedic was the third, being commissioned in 1909. The three lighthouse keepers and their families lived an isolated existence, receiving supplies only four times each year.

Right: In this 15-minute time exposure the swirling waters of the Southern Ocean are coloured with the cool hues of dawn.

D R Y L A N D S   W E T L A N D S

▶ The Stuart Highway is a 2716 kilometre umbilical cord which dissects Australia into east and west halves. Once a mere track laden with 'bulldust' and full of pot holes, it took weeks to negotiate. These days the highway is a wide, well surfaced road, the domain of 'road trains' which transport everything from cattle to paper clips from one end of the continent to the other. From Port Augusta in the south to Darwin in the north, the Stuart Highway takes you through some of the most arid regions of the continent, where rain may not fall for years, and up to the tropics, where the storms of the wet season flood the rivers and close the roads.

▶ After leaving Port Augusta the first town of any size is Coober Pedy, opal centre of Australia, 540 kilometres to the north. Ironically, it was the search for gold which led to opals being found in this desolate region. In 1915, young Bill Hutchinson was accompanying his father on a gold-seeking expedition, but as they headed north from Naracoorte the party was hampered by a severe drought and the need to find water took priority over their search for gold. With Bill left to mind the camp, the other members of the party dispersed to search for water, returning at dusk to find Bill gone. With the last light he strolled back into camp, not only having found water to last several days, but opal floaters (lumps of opal found on the surface) as well. Over the next few days the party gathered many more floaters, while continuing their vain search for water. Finding none, they were forced to return to Adelaide. News of their find soon spread and several groups set out to try to locate the Hutchinson field. All failed until Jim and Dick O'Neill, opal miners from Lightning Ridge, eventually found an area covered with opal floaters. Nine months later the brothers returned to Adelaide with opal valued in excess of £17,000, a fortune back then.

▶ The area became known as the Stuarts Range Opal field and prospectors were drawn from all over the world to its hot and dusty environs in the hope of making their fortune. By 1925 Stuarts Range had a population of more than 500 and had been renamed Coober Pedy, an Aboriginal name which, roughly translated, means 'white fellas hole in the ground', because of the preference for its inhabitants to live underground. They do this not only to escape the searing heat of summer and the bitter chill of winter nights, but because there is so little building material to be found on this barren, treeless landscape in the Great Victoria Desert. Coober Pedy's population has waxed and waned over the years with the changing price of opal, but these days it has in excess of 2000 residents and is one of the most multicultural towns in Australia.

▶ In an area which receives less than 100 mm of rain annually there were times in the early days of Coober Pedy when water was almost as precious as opal, and was rationed to a mere 15 litres per day. These days Coober Pedy boasts a modern solar still which converts the hot, salt-laden water of the artesian basin into beautiful drinking water.

▶ Water, or the lack of it, hampered many expeditions into central Australia. There had been three consecutive years of drought and seven years of below average rainfall when Harold Bell Lasseter set out from Alice Springs in July 1930 to try and find a reef of gold he claimed to have originally discovered in the Petermann Ranges 33 years earlier. Lasseter, as a young man of 17 was prospecting for rubies when he came across a reef in which, "The yellow stuff was thick as plums in a pudding". He very nearly perished from dehydration after making his find and was fortunate to be rescued by a camel driver who took him to safety. A gold boom during the early years of this century saw the opening of many new goldfields and Lasseter was unable to interest anyone in financing an expedition to the remote and rugged regions of central Australia until 1930. By then, production from the existing goldfields had slowed, and Australia's economy was sliding further into recession. Lasseter was able to gain sponsorship from influential people such as members of government and leaders of industry to locate his reef of gold, which they felt had the potential to solve Australia's financial crisis.

▶ By July 21st 1930 Lasseter was on his way back to the Petermann Ranges with a well equipped expedition which included a car, a truck and a plane. But in spite of being well financed and provisioned, the expedition was plagued by problems from the start. Many of the usual water holes were dry because of the drought, the vehicles had difficulty negotiating the terrain and the plane crashed before it had served any useful purpose. The conflicting personalities within the group led to fights, mistrust and suspicion and the eventual disintegration of the party. By mid-October they were no closer to finding the reef than when they started and relations had deteriorated to such a degree that Lasseter found himself continuing the search alone with only two camels for company. Legend has it, that as he relieved himself in the bushes, the camels were spooked (some say by the noise Lasseter was making!) and bolted. Although he was able to retrieve some provisions thrown off by the animals in their panic, Lasseter was in a desperate situation. Already suffering from dysentery, he was lucky to be found by two Aboriginal hunters, who took him to their cave on Boomerang Creek. His health failed to improve during the weeks he stayed there, waiting in vain for a rescue party to find him. An entry in Lasseter's diary at that time reads, "What good a reef worth millions. I would give it all for a loaf of bread." In late January 1931 he decided to make an attempt to reach the expedition's base camp at Ilpili and left the cave, heading east along the Petermann Ranges. For 25 kilometres he walked through the bush to Irving Creek but by this stage he was so weak he could go no further. Sadly, Lasseter died there some days later but the legend of his gold reef lives on.

▶ Aboriginal people had lived in central Australia for at least 10,000 years when Ayers Rock was first discovered by Europeans in 1873. The permanent water supply of Mutitjulu (Maggie Springs) at the base of the rock, and the wildlife it attracted made it possible for the local Anangu people to live there for extended periods. The Anangu believe that Ayers Rock and the Olgas were created and shaped into their present forms during the Tjukurpa (Dreamtime) period, and all the physical features of the rock represent various activities of ancestral beings.

▶ One Dreamtime story tells of two snakes, Kuniya a python and Liru a poisonous snake. Kuniya became angry when her nephew Liru failed to behave in a respectful way. As Kuniya approached Liru, she was so angry that she picked up a handful of sand and let it fall to the ground to settle the forces she was disturbing so no harm would come to others. Kuniya then struck Liru, who deflected the blow with his shield but when Kuniya struck him a second time he received a deep and fatal wound. From Maggie Springs Kuniya can be seen as a thick, wriggling, horizontal band of rock high on the face of Uluru as she moves in to attack Liru, and the sand she let fall can be seen as the roughened cavity beneath her.

▶ Fire was just as important to the Aboriginal inhabitants of Australia as water and its use in cooking, hunting and clearing the land dates back thousands of years. Not only did fire flush animals from hiding, but it cleared pathways through the bush. The practice of burning early in the dry season promoted the growth of new shoots and reduced the amount of fuel available in the event of a lightning strike. The widespread use of controlled burning continues in the north to this day. Despite this, many thousands of hectares are frequently ravaged by bushfires.

Like the mounds of a thousand ant colonies, the tailings of the opal mines at Coober Pedy, in South Australia are silhouetted by the setting sun. This multi-coloured stone was first discovered in the region as 'floaters' (lumps of opal on the surface), but these days shafts are sunk to extract it. To escape the relentless summer heat, many of the residents of Coober Pedy live underground and the town even boasts an underground motel!

Previous page: Its years of service over, and with paintwork peeling and faded by the desert sun, a 1940 Ford 1 Ton Ute sits patiently awaiting its ultimate fate.

The stunning colours of sunset profile a desert oak. Vibrant sunsets and clear, star studded skies are a feature of a visit to the Outback.

Overleaf: The spectacle of the rich, warm colours of Uluru (Ayers Rock) at sunset attracts visitors from around the world.

Pages 50-51: Framed by the desert she-oaks, the mighty bulk of Uluru, in central Australia rises abruptly from the surrounding plain.

Pages 52-53: During this five-hour time exposure, the brilliant stars of the desert sky trace their arc through the heavens.

Left: The impressive amphitheatre of Kalarranga Valley in the Finke Gorge National Park of central Australia.

Previous pages: Known as Kata Tjuta (place of many heads) to the Aboriginal people, the Olgas are located in Uluru National Park and are visible from the summit of Ayers Rock.

Below: The beautifully coloured rainbow bee-eater, which feeds on a variety of venomous winged insects, is found throughout the drier Australian woodlands. The bee-eater captures its prey on the wing, flying back to a perch to squeeze out any sting before eating.

The tall red *Livistona mariae* cabbage palm of Palm Valley is one of the rarest trees in the world. A remnant of a wetter era, when rainforest thrived in central Australia, this palm has adapted to an increasingly arid environment.

Left: A permanent waterhole on Ormiston Creek in the West MacDonnell Ranges of central Australia. The local Aranda people believe the waterhole is inhabited by a great watersnake.

Right: Fracturing the rock with tenacious roots, this ghost gum has ensured its survival by reaching deeply to the water table below.

Previous pages: The colourful ochre pits of the West MacDonnell Ranges are a traditional source of pigment for the Aboriginal people of the region. As well as being used in local ceremonies, the ochre was an important item of trade.

Left: Ormiston Gorge and Pound, in the West MacDonnell Ranges, is a popular destination for both bushwalkers and sightseers. Nimble rock wallabies are frequently seen on the steep sides of the gorge, and the permanent waterhole pictured here offers one of the few fish-breeding habitats of central Australia.

Right: The smooth white bark of a ghost gum offers a striking contrast to its dusty surrounds. A feature of arid Australia, the pure bark and twisted shapes of the ghost gums have inspired artists such as Albert Namatjira and Sidney Nolan.

Left: Cleft by thundering floodwaters of past ages, the towering walls of Standley Chasm reflect the glow of the midday sun. Located in the West MacDonnell Ranges, the Chasm is only 50 kilometres west of Alice Springs.

Right: Its twin trunks intertwined, a ghost gum seeks shelter in the lee of one of the huge granite boulders known as the Devil's Marbles. Located 420 kilometres north of Alice Springs, these rare formations are the result of weathering. The original granite mass first broke into rectangular blocks along joint lines, which were gradually rounded to egg shapes by erosion and flaking of the surface layers.

Overleaf: Glowing in the setting sun, the Devil's Marbles are an important Aboriginal site. These spherical boulders represent eggs laid by the Rainbow Serpent during the Dreamtime.

Seasonal burning of the undergrowth has been a part of the annual cycle for the inhabitants of northern Australia for thousands of years. In addition to reducing the amount of fuel available in the event of a wildfire, the practice of burning encourages the growth of new shoots. In stark contrast to the controlled burning, bushfires such as this one frequently damage large areas of the north.

As the fire raged, aided by strong winds, crows and kites circled overhead feeding on insects, reptiles and small mammals trying to escape the flames. Kites have been seen picking up a firebrand in their beaks to restart a dying fire, presumably for the feed that is flushed out.

A male common crow butterfly rests on a pandanus leaf.

A pelican makes its laborious take-off from a mist-shrouded billabong in Kakadu, in the Top End of the Northern Territory. One of the most popular parks in Australia, Kakadu has World Heritage status on the basis of both its natural features and its cultural significance.

Offering a panoramic view over the floodplains of the East Alligator River, Ubirr Rock, in Kakadu National Park, is a popular site for watching the sunset. A sandstone outlier of the Arnhem Land Plateau, Ubirr has traditionally been favoured by the Aboriginal inhabitants because of the rich variety of foods found locally. The nearby river, swamps and woodlands provide such delicacies as yam, wallaby, goanna, echidna, fish, mussels and waterfowl.

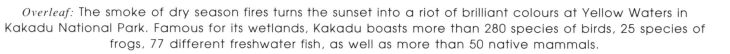

The short walk to the summit of Ubirr passes magnificent Aboriginal art sites and groves of pandanus before the final scramble to the top. More than 120 rock painting sites are recorded in the rock shelters of the Ubirr area and several feature now-extinct animals such as the thylacine (Tasmanian tiger).

Overleaf: The smoke of dry season fires turns the sunset into a riot of brilliant colours at Yellow Waters in Kakadu National Park. Famous for its wetlands, Kakadu boasts more than 280 species of birds, 25 species of frogs, 77 different freshwater fish, as well as more than 50 native mammals.

The beautiful Maguk waterhole in the drier southern section of Kakadu. With no threat of saltwater crocodiles, which can be dangerous predators of humans, Maguk is a popular swimming hole, although freshwater crocodiles do inhabit its waters. Feeding on fish, frogs, lizards, snakes and other small animals, the freshwater crocodile grows to a maximum size of 3 metres and is distinguishable from its more dangerous saltwater relative by a narrower snout and the four large scales across the neck.

Red lilies line the banks of the East Alligator River in Arnhem Land. A favoured food of the Aboriginal people, water lily bulbs are harvested by wading into waters inhabited by the saltwater crocodile. In 1976 the Arnhem Land region was returned to its traditional owners, with the Kakadu area later being declared as a national park.

The awesome saltwater crocodile inhabits tidal rivers as well as freshwater waterways. Growing to more than 5 metres in length, it feeds mostly on fish, but has also been responsible for several human deaths.

The delicate jacana is also known as the 'Jesus Bird', due to its apparent ability to walk on water, though actually it walks on water plants as it forages amongst the vegetation for seeds and insects.

An inhabitant of Australia's north and east coasts, the jabiru (or black-necked stork), stalks its prey of fish, frogs and crabs in the shallows of freshwater swamps and billabongs.

At the commencement of the wet season, magpie geese flock to Kakadu in their thousands, to mate. Their resonant honking can be heard across vast distances.

Barely a ripple disturbs the tranquillity of Yellow Waters, on the South Alligator River. Well populated with saltwater crocodiles, the three main rivers of Kakadu were mistakenly named 'Alligator' by early British explorers. Although no alligators exist in Australia, the name remains.

The soft light of dusk paints the distant ranges in hues of pink and magenta in the Keep River National Park. Situated on the Northern Territory's western border, Keep River features several important rock art sites, including Nganalang (or Cockatoo Dreaming), a large rock shelter which is split by an archway. The Dreamtime story says that Nganalang, the white cockatoo lady, poked her nose bone through the rock, making the hole. Unusual beehive-shaped rock formations like those found in this park are also found in the Bungle Bungles and the Hidden Valley National Park, both in Western Australia.

T H E   W I D E   W E S T

▶ Crossing the border into Western Australia is a bit like entering another country; it's just so big. Even the maps we were using changed scale, so it seemed as though we travelled for hours before making any progress across the page. That sort of space appeals to some people; there's an inherent freedom in the sight of plains stretching from horizon to horizon without so much as a roofline to interrupt the transition from earth to sky. The vast expanses of the west were among the last to be opened up by Europeans, and many areas remain remote and isolated to this day.

▶ The Kimberley region, in the far north of Western Australia, epitomises this isolation. The area remained virtually uninhabited until the legendary stockman and drover Nat 'Bluey' Buchanan paved the way for cattle farming in the region. He must have made a comical sight in the middle of the outback: a man astride a camel, holding a green umbrella over his head! Of Irish extraction, with fair complexion, Bluey needed his umbrella for protection against the fierce Australian sun as he pioneered the route which the Duracks and others later followed to bring their cattle west. Yet there was nothing comical about his achievements. A spare man who never smoked or drank alcohol, Nat Buchanan pioneered many of the great droving routes of the Australian outback, including the stock route to the Murchison. At the age of 70 he was still droving when the South Australian Government supplied him with camels to find a more direct route from north Queensland across to Western Australia! He always sipped just one pint of water a day, even when in civilisation, to keep himself in training for his next venture. A man of vision, he established the vast Wave Hill Station in the Northern Territory and instigated the export of beef to Singapore, from the Kimberley port of Derby.

▶ By the early years of the twentieth century there were many who had followed Nat Buchanan, the Duracks and others into the Kimberley. They lived an isolated existence, without any means of communication other than the infrequent mail service and the bush telegraph. Between their distant outposts rode another man on a camel, bringing friendship, medical assistance and pastoral care. Although he lacked Nat Buchanan's eccentricity of appearance, there were those who called him mad, because he had a dream. He dreamed of a day when the people of the bush wouldn't be so isolated, when the women didn't die in childbirth because the doctor couldn't get to them in time, when young children wouldn't die from meningitis or influenza before they could reach medical help, when miners wouldn't die from malaria through a lack of quinine.

▶ That man was John Flynn and such was his enthusiasm that the Australian Inland Mission was formed and public donations started to flow. By 1925 hospitals had been built at Oodnadatta and Beltana in South Australia, Port Hedland and Halls Creek in Western Australia, Maranboy in the Northern Territory and Birdsville in south western Queensland. Between them rode travelling padres whose 'parishes' covered thousands of square kilometres. After the padres came the 'boundary riders', nursing sisters on horseback who moved from station to station, providing medical assistance wherever it was required. But John Flynn was still troubled and saw that radios and aeroplanes were needed to overcome the problem of isolation. The idea of the Royal Flying Doctor Service (RFDS) was born, but the technology was not yet available to make Flynn's dream a reality. Three years later, in 1928, the first RFDS base was opened at Cloncurry in Queensland, but it was to be some years before every outpost station would have a two-way radio. In the first 12 months of operation, the Royal Flying Doctor Service flew 32,000 kilometres, attending to 255 patients. In 1929 the first pedal-operated radios, which utilised a keyboard to send a morse signal, were being installed and by the mid 1930s voice radios were in widespread use. Through the vision of one man and the hard work and dedication of thousands of others, John Flynn's dream had become a reality and the people of the outback were able to summon help in an emergency.

▶ Over the years the system has evolved to include services such as the 'School of the Air', through which children in remote areas supplement their correspondence notes with daily lessons on the radio. In the 1930s an interconnected RFDS radio-telecom service was established which enabled outpost stations to transmit and receive telephone calls.

▶ Although the communications role of the RFDS is diminishing as telecommunications technology advances, the emergency and healthcare role of the RFDS continues. In 1993 the RFDS attended some 153,000 people and its 37 aircraft flew 8,900,000 kilometres, providing over 14,000 evacuations. It is the most comprehensive aerial healthcare service in the world, looking after the well-being of people in an area of 6,900,000 square kilometres!

▶ It was problems with the radio which forced Charles Kingsford-Smith's plane, the *Southern Cross* down in the Kimberley region in 1929. Having made history by being the first to cross the Pacific the previous year, the Australian air ace and his 3 crew were en-route to Wyndham, from where they were to attempt the world's first aerial circumnavigation. The aerial for their radio was knocked from the plane as the navigator Litchfield was taking a sight on the sun. Consequently, they didn't receive a message which had been telegraphed to Sydney from Wyndham soon after their departure, advising them to delay their take-off as dust storms were sweeping across the Western Australian desert. After crossing the tropic of Capricorn north west of Alice Springs the plane encountered a violent electrical storm and the predicted dust, which reduced visibility to almost zero. Lashing rain followed, turning the dust to a sticky ochre that smeared across the windshield and the compass began to behave erratically. By dawn the weather had eased somewhat but they were uncertain of their position. Before they could establish their where-abouts with accuracy, they began to lose power and 'Smithy' was forced to make an emergency landing in the Kimberley.

▶ The moment they were safely on the ground they took stock of their position, discovering to their alarm that the emergency food locker was empty save for some coffee, a packet of biscuits and some brandy. As they drank their first cup of coffee, mixed with a quarter of the brandy, Smithy held his cup aloft and said, "Well, mates, we may be lost, but at least we've got coffee royal to drink".

▶ Little did they know that as soon as the news of their mishap became known, the *Smiths Weekly*, an influential paper of the time, published the story that the forced landing was a publicity stunt. During the search for the *Southern Cross* two pilots, Hitchcock and Anderson died in the desert after a forced landing. The event became known as the 'Coffee Royal Affair' and public opinion turned against Kingsford-Smith and his crew, even though they were later exonerated by a committee of enquiry into the incident. On their return to Sydney they received an acrimonious reception, which was in striking contrast to the jubilant welcome given after the completion of the trans-Pacific flight only one year earlier.

▶ Not very far from where the *Southern Cross* went down runs the dusty and corrugated Kalumburu Road, which heads north from the Gibb River Road into the northernmost part of the Kimberley. In spite of planes, radio and modern telecommunications, the people who live in this remote region remain isolated by any city dweller's standards. 'Town' is either Kununurra or Derby, which are more than 350 dusty kilometres away. During the dry, one or the other is visited a couple of times for supplies, while emergency provisions are brought in on the mail plane's weekly visit. During the wet the stations are isolated by floodwaters much of the time. To receive their education, the children either go to boarding school or participate in the 'School of the Air'. Although it seems a tough and isolated existence, few would admit to loneliness. Seeing nature operate on such a grand scale, with the incredible extremes of the storms of the wet season and the shimmering mirages of the dry season, it's not difficult to understand how such a life gets under the skin.

The classic beehive-shaped domes of the Bungle Bungles in the Kimberley region of Western Australia are extremely fragile multi-hued formations of sandstone laid down in the Devonian era some 350 million years ago. The alternating horizontal bands of light and dark sediments, reflecting changes in the water content of the layers, are accentuated by protective skins of silica and lichen which have developed to create the striking contrast of orange and black.

Previous page: Swaying grasses of the dry season in the Bungle Bungles region of the Kimberley. Known as Purnululu to the Aboriginal people, the region was discovered by Europeans in 1879 but then largely forgotten until recent times. It was declared a national park in 1987.

The best view of the domes of the Bungle Bungles is undoubtedly from the air, where the extent of these unique formations can best be appreciated. With no obstruction to hinder the view, a helicopter flight offers the thrill of a lifetime as you fly over the beehives and along the gorges, almost skimming the tree-tops along the way.

A visitor to Mini Palms Gorge in the Bungle Bungles is dwarfed by the towering walls of the gorge. On the floor of the chasm, small palms grow in neat configuration as though planted by a divine hand. The gorge is a welcome refuge from the scorching heat outside where temperatures exceeding 40^0 C are not uncommon. At the far extremity of the gorge, a cave penetrates the rockface.

Right: Deep within Mini Palms Gorge, *Livistona* palms reach up towards the light, their slender trunks swaying gently in the light breeze.

Below: The frill-necked lizard's formidable claws make it adept at tree-climbing. The lizard's famous frill varies in colour from region to region and is used in territorial displays as well as to deter attacks. One of the largest dragon lizards, a mature male can measure almost 90 centimetres in length. An anti-bushfire slogan in the north says, 'We like our lizards frilled, not grilled'.

●*Left:* A section of the corrugated and dusty Kalumburu Road, in the Kimberley region of Western Australia. Lined with *Livistona* palms, the road leads north off the famous Gibb River Road, to Mitchell Falls and the Aboriginal community of Kalumburu.

●*Right:* Windjana Gorge is part of a giant reef of Devonian limestone, which formed under the sea about 350 million years ago. Its sheer walls now rise more than 50 metres above the surrounding plain and have been coloured and furrowed by the onslaught of wet season rains. Packed with marine fossils which pre-date the evolution of reptiles and mammals, Windjana Gorge is the finest example of a fossilised barrier reef to be found anywhere in the world.

Gantheaume Point, with its richly textured rock formations, offers a distant view to Cable Beach, near Broome in the north of Western Australia. Cable Beach is so named because it was the site of a telegraphic link with Java. Its 22 kilometres of white sand and turquoise water today attract visitors from all over the world.

Its striking azure blue colour is a feature of the Indian Ocean at Eighty Mile Beach, approximately halfway between Broome and Port Hedland. The rising tide brings a bounty to anglers, as thread-fin salmon come to feed in the shallows.

Marooned by the receding tide, a colourful collection of shells decorates the beach.

The wet sand of an outgoing tide mirrors the silver light of the rising moon. At low tide the beach is hundreds of metres wide and the receding waters reveal thousands of beautiful shells.

Above the high water mark the sand is sculptured into ridges by the constant breeze.

Overleaf lower right: A spinifex pigeon searches the stony ground for seed. One of the few birds to reside permanently in the arid grasslands of central and northern Australia, the spinifex pigeon is well adapted to living there at all times. Its low metabolic rate reduces the bird's food requirements and the amount of water needed to cool its body. Its diet consists almost entirely of seeds, notably those of spinifex grass.

Left: A cool waterfall slices between layers of hot rock at Hamersley Gorge in the Pilbara region of Western Australia.

Right: Deep within Dales Gorge, in the Karajini (Hamersley Range) National Park, the waters of Circular Pool look cool and inviting. Accessible for only a small part of its 40-kilometre length the gorge is bordered by tall cliffs topped with ghost gums.

Left: The classic bottle-shaped boab trees, which drop their leaves in the dry season to conserve valuable moisture, are a feature of northern Australia.

Right: The bare branches of a young boab tree contrast with the sweeping waves of layered rock at Hamersley Gorge.

Below: A female blue-winged kooka-burra surveys the scene with amusement. Famed for its diet of snakes and lizards, the kookaburra actually survives largely on insects and other invertebrates.

This hardy desert perennial holds perilously to a crumbling wall of Joffre Gorge, in the iron ore-rich Hamersley Range. Hamersley Iron commenced mining iron ore in the region in the 1960s after the Commonwealth government lifted an export embargo. The embargo had been in place since 1938, when it was thought that Australia had only 50 million tonne of iron ore left. When the Mount Tom Price deposit was discovered in the region in 1962, it was estimated to contain 900 million tonne of iron ore!

In contrast to the deep gorges which dissect the landscape, the Pilbara region is also characterised by rocky outcrops interspersed with golden tussocks of spinifex. Receiving a mere 300 mm of rainfall annually, this arid environment supports only the hardiest vegetation. The rain falls mostly in summer, as tropical downpours, and much of it quickly evaporates. For most of the year fresh water is found only in isolated pools.

The Hamersley Iron Road disappears from sight on the way to Millstream Chichester National Park. Leading to the springs of the Millstream oasis, on the Fortescue River, the road follows the iron ore railway and water pipeline. Water from the springs is piped to the towns of Karratha, Dampier, Roebourne and Wickham.

Part of the Millstream oasis, near the old homestead and property which also bear that name. At its peak the Millstream station covered over 400,000 hectares and carried 55,000 head of sheep. An extensive market garden was worked by eleven Chinese gardeners, and the date and cotton palms which now line the waterways are a legacy of that era.

Situated north of Carnarvon, on the Western Australian coast, the boiling surf of Point Quobba has claimed many lives. Treacherous 'king' waves have frequently swept unwary anglers and sightseers from the rocks.

The limestone sentinels of the Pinnacles Desert rise from a stark landscape of yellow sand in Nambung National Park, 250 kilometres north of Perth. Thought by Dutch sailors to be the remains of an ancient city the Pinnacles are in fact the eroded remnants of what was once a thick bed of limestone beneath the coastal sand dunes.

Rugged windswept heaths and sheltered bays characterise the Torndirrup National Park on the south coast of Western Australia. This perched granite boulder overlooks the rolling swells of the Southern Ocean.

Known locally as Murphy's Haystacks, these residual lumps of granite, or inselbergs, are located on the Eyre Peninsula near Streaky Bay in South Australia. Their name was acquired after an Irish agriculturalist, who advocated harrowing the land to produce good hay, noticed the formations in the distance as he passed by on the coach. Thinking them to be enormous stacks of hay, he informed the driver and other passengers that the farmer must harrow his land to produce so much hay! Being located on Murphy's property they soon became known as Murphy's Haystacks.

DESERT DWELLERS

▶ There were many early British explorers and settlers who believed that Australia must have a fertile heart; they couldn't conceive of such a vast land having only deserts in its interior. As we left Adelaide and headed north for the second time on our journey we were drawn northeast into the heart of the South Australian desert, where, in one of the most tragic episodes in Australian history, the explorers Burke and Wills perished after crossing the continent from south to north. Although they died on Coopers Creek, in South Australia's far north-west their expedition and those of the people who went in search of them added much to the knowledge of central Australia and opened up large tracts of land to farming and grazing.

▶ It was some three months after their enthusiastic farewell from Melbourne on August 20th 1860, that John O'Hara Burke arrived at Coopers Creek, in the north east of South Australia. Keen to move faster than his large expedition allowed, Burke had forged ahead from Menindee with 8 men, 16 camels and 15 horses, to set up their camp. Although forced to move from their first location by a plague of rats they subsequently set camp further along the creek beside what was to become Australia's most famous coolibah tree, which they marked with their depot number LXV. With plenty of water and abundant fish, mussels and birds the party spent a relaxing month waiting for the following members of the party. When they hadn't arrived by December 16th, Burke decided to push on into the expanses of Sturt's Stony Desert with Wills, King and Gray leaving Brahe in charge of the men remaining at the depot. Brahe's instructions were to build a stockade and to wait for three months until their return.

▶ In spite of the heat, the decision must have seemed justified at first, because they made good progress. The previous winter had been wet and there was adequate water and plenty of feed for the stock all through the desert. But by the time they reached the tropics, it was mid January and the torrential rains and humidity of the wet season soon slowed their progress and sapped their energy. Fifty kilometres from the coast, Burke and Wills left Gray, King and the camels at depot CXIX and went on alone. On February 11th, Burke and Wills camped beside a creek which had a twenty centimetre tide. They had crossed the continent and reached the Gulf but were denied the sight of the open ocean by mangrove swamps which barred their way. Nevertheless, success was theirs.

▶ With two thirds of their supplies exhausted they now faced the arduous return journey. The driving rain of the tropics slowed their progress and by the time they reached the desert they were in extremely bad shape. On April 17th Gray died and the men were so weak it took all day to dig a grave in which to bury him. The next day they set out to cover the final 112 kilometres of Sturt's Stony Desert with no food and very little water.

▶ It was April 21st when the party staggered back to depot LXV only to find it deserted. Although Brahe's instructions had been to wait there for three months, he had waited an extra month before finally giving Burke, Wills, Gray and King up for dead. In one of the cruelest cases of bad timing in Australian history, Brahe left the Cooper only nine hours before the three exhausted men returned. Before leaving, Brahe had buried supplies and emblazoned the depot tree with the message 'DIG 3 FT. N.W. APR 21 1861'. The 'Dig Tree', as it subsequently became known, is the most famous tree in Australian history.

▶ Two days after retrieving the buried supplies, Burke, Wills and King left the depot and headed down the Cooper, leaving the river a few kilometres south of the present-day town of Innamincka. After walking more than 70 kilometres into the desert they realised their position was hopeless and they returned to the Cooper, where Burke and Wills died two months later. The last words written by Burke were, "I hope we shall be done justice. We fulfilled our task but we were not followed up as expected and the depot party abandoned their post". King was nursed by Aborigines until a rescue party found him in mid September.

▶ It was only 10 years after the Burke and Wills tragedy that the infamous Harry

Redford pioneered the nearby Strzelecki Track, when he drove 1000 head of stolen cattle along it. Although undoubtedly a thief, Redford was no ordinary cattle duffer. A renowned stockman and drover, he conceived a daring plan to muster 1000 head of cattle off the enormous Bowen Downs Station in central Queensland and drive them along the Barcoo River to Strzelecki Creek. His ultimate destination was Adelaide, where he intended to pass himself off as an overlander from Queensland and sell the mob.

▶ Having built yards in a remote section of the Bowen Downs property, he and a couple of cohorts succeeded in mustering their 1000 head and set off down the Barcoo. Upon reaching the junction of the Cooper they crossed near the famous 'Dig Tree', before proceeding down Strzelecki Creek. Stopping briefly at Wallelderdine Station, they were relieved to exchange a distinctive white bull for some stores before resuming their journey south. They didn't have to continue on to Adelaide as planned, because at Blanchewater Station they were offered £5,000 for the whole mob, which they accepted. Even so, they had driven the cattle more than 2000 kilometres and in so doing had opened up a new stock route across the continent.

▶ Harry Redford eventually came to trial for his misdemeanors; the white bull and one of his companions had betrayed him. By this time he had achieved the status of folk hero and the trial, which was held in the Roma district court in Queensland, attracted much interest. In a wonderful piece of bush justice and in spite of conclusive evidence, the jury failed to convict him, reputedly because they admired his feats as a stockman and drover. The judge was furious and was moved to comment, "I thank God that verdict is yours, gentlemen and not mine".

▶ In spite of his cattle duffing exploits Harry Redford was subsequently chosen to overland 3000 head of cattle from the Barcoo River to the newly discovered Barkly Tableland, where he founded and managed Brunette Downs station. During the 1880s his drives from the Atherton Tableland to Dubbo earned him a reputation alongside Nat Buchanan and Patrick Durack as one of the three great drovers of the north until his premature death by drowning in Corella Creek in the Northern Territory in 1901.

▶ Our search for one of Australia's living legends took us next to Molly Clark's Old Andado Station, nestled between red sand dunes on the fringe of the Simpson Desert. A legend in her own lifetime (though she wouldn't agree), Molly came to Andado in 1955 as a 28 eight year old. No stranger to the bush, Molly was governess at Mungeranie, on the Birdsville Track, when she married Mac Clark, a ringer on the station. Together, they went on to manage three properties in the region before they were offered a half share of the 7500 square kilometre Andado Station.

▶ Molly arrived at Andado to find that the 'homestead' was a corrugated iron shack of four rooms, which still had an earth floor. She and Mac brought up three sons there and over the years they turned the cattle station into a profitable concern. By 1960 they were able to move out of the shack and into a new homestead they'd built nearby. But, like so many of the stories of the bush, there came a period of tragedy. In Molly's case this began in the late 1970s. First Mac died of a heart attack only hours after surviving a light plane crash, then one of Molly's sons was killed in a road accident. Just a few years later the station had to be de-stocked in line with the government's policy of eradicating tuberculosis and brucellosis from cattle. In 1985 Molly and her remaining sons cut their losses and moved up to 'town' (Alice Springs). But she wasn't there for long; the red sandhills of the Simpson were beckoning and Molly set about planning her return, eventually persuading the Northern Territory government to grant her freehold to 45 square kilometres of the property, including the old homestead. Molly had restored the old shack and stacked it with bush memorabilia during 1972 and these days she gives passing travellers a taste of how the bush was pioneered. On Mother's Day in 1993 she opened the National Pioneer Women's Hall of Fame at the homestead, in recognition of the unsung heroes of the Australian bush, the women like herself who played such an important role in the outback.

●The stone ramparts of Wilpena Pound in South Australia's Flinders Ranges, catch the first rays of the sun. Eighteen kilometres long and 8 kilometres wide, the pound is encircled by walls of erosion-resistant sedimentary rock, rich in quartzite. Less resistant rocks such as mud-stone and shale where eroded to form the central plain. Wilpena, an Aboriginal word meaning 'place of bent fingers', (probably in reference to the pound's resemblance to a cupped hand), was an important ceremonial site until the middle of last century.

●*Previous page:* Like the old telegraph station nearby, this dead tree will soon be buried by the shifting sands of Eucla on the Great Australian Bight.

Right: Inside the rustic 1850s shearing shed on Angorichina Station, in the northern Flinders Ranges. Built entirely of hand-sawn timbers and corrugated iron, the shed stands as testimony to the industry of early farmers in the region. The timber is mostly local pine and the corrugated iron for the roof came from England as ship's ballast.

Left: A collection of farming artefacts inside the Angorichina shearing shed.

Below: The shearing season over for another year, a wool basket stands empty until the next clip.

The apparently desolate plains of saltbush and bluebush west of Port Augusta, on the Eyre Peninsula in South Australia, yield fine quality merino wool. Here, Don and Lachlan Nicolson of Roopena Station sort out a 'woollie' from the flock during muster.

The light of the rising moon and setting sun colour these dead gums in ghostly hues.

Left and Right: Wind-sculptured dunes alongside the Strzelecki Track. The track was pioneered in 1870 by the infamous cattle duffer Harry Redford, who with three friends, drove 1000 stolen cattle down the Strzelecki Creek.
A roller-coaster road across near-parallel dune ridges heading east from here leads to Cameron's Corner, where the boarders of New South Wales, South Australia and Queensland meet.

Below: A wrought-iron signpost on the Strzelecki Track.

Despite their lifeless appearance the dunes play host to an enormous variety of reptiles and other animals, which find shelter in their sparse vegetation or in their cooler depths. Mostly nocturnal creatures, their delicate footprints are the only sign of their passing.

Sculptured by the prevailing winds, the red colouration of the dunes is caused by a coating of iron oxide on the sand grains. After rain, the dunes are carpeted with colourful flowers, which complete their life cycle within just a few weeks.

Above left: The famous Burke and Wills 'Dig Tree' or cache number 65 (LXV), on the Cooper River near the town of Innamincka. After succeeding in their epic attempt to cross Australia from south to north in 1860-1861, Burke, Wills and a companion King, arrived back at this camp exhausted, only to find it deserted. With the explorers already a month overdue, their base camp companions had left only hours before, having given them up for dead. Nevertheless, they had buried supplies for the explorers, marking the spot with the word 'dig' on this tree. The dig instructions have long since grown over and all that remains visible now are the carved Roman numerals.

Above right: On an adjacent tree is a portrait of Burke, carved in 1898.

Sturt's Stony Desert, which Burke and Wills traversed on their epic journey, is typified by wide expanses of gibber, interspersed with mesas and buttes. On the explorer's journey north in late 1860 the desert was well grassed as a result of unusually good winter rains, allowing the stock to remain in excellent condition, but by the time of their return in April 1861 conditions were not so favourable. One of their companions, Gray, and most of the animals had died, and the remaining party of Burke, Wills and King had to complete the 112 kilometre desert crossing with no food and only a little water.

The domed roof of this old sheep shearing shed is characteristic of the buildings on Cordillo Downs Station in far north-eastern South Australia. On the flat gibber plains of the region, wood is a scarce commodity and a method of construction which minimised the use of roofing timbers was sought. The solution was this domed, corrugated iron roof structure, supported by buttressed stone walls more than half-a-metre thick.

By 1883 this seemingly inhospitable landscape supported 10,000 sheep, with the number increasing to over 85,000 by the turn of the century. Shearers caught the train to Lyndhurst, some 600 kilometres to the south, then cycled the rest of the way! The wool clip was transported by Afghan camel train to Farina, on the Central Australian Railway, 50 kilometres south of Marree.

This small stone hut on Cordillo Downs seems to have grown out of the stony ground from which it was constructed. Although Cordillo was well suited to running sheep, predation by dingoes eventually forced a change to cattle in 1941. These days the station runs about 8000 head on an area in excess of 700 square kilometres.

A meeting point for tourists and locals, the Birdsville pub's special 'seven-course-meal', is guaranteed to quench even the fiercest thirst!

An impressive array of bush lore adorns the pub's walls, including these stockmen's hats.

The Birdsville Pub, in far south-western Queensland is an icon of the Australian bush. Situated on the eastern edge of the Simpson Desert, it is a welcome sight for travellers who have just crossed some 1100 red sand dunes. Starting out as a depot for surveyors working in the Simpson, by 1890 the town had three hotels, three general stores, two blacksmiths and a school. These days it is famous for the annual Birdsville Races, its one remaining hotel and its isolation.

At 578 metres, Algebuckina Bridge on the Central Australian Railway is the longest bridge in South Australia. It was originally planned that the railway would link Adelaide with Darwin, but Oodnadatta remained the northernmost station from 1890 until 1929. In such an arid environment, it is ironic that water forced the eventual closure of the line. Flash floods caused great damage and eventually repairs became too expensive. Local folklore has it that the wrecked car beneath Algebuckina Bridge was attempting to use the rail bridge to cross the flooded creek when it was pushed off by an oncoming train.

Now in ruins, Wangianna Station on the Oodnadatta Track was once an important watering point for the thirsty steam engines of the Central Australian Railway. The planned rail link to Darwin never eventuated, although the line was extended as far as Alice Springs in 1929. Before then, Afghan cameleers and their 'ships of the desert' ferried goods and passengers north from Oodnadatta. In honour of these hardy pioneers, the nickname 'the Ghan' was applied to trains travelling along the line.

In the isolated town of Oodnadatta, the Pink
Roadhouse rests quietly in the dawn light.
Later in the day the roadhouse will be a
thriving centre of activity for locals and
tourists alike. Good artesian water was found
when the township was surveyed in 1890 in
preparation for the extension of the railhead
from Warrina. Until the railway pushed through
to Alice Springs in 1929, Oodnadatta was an
important inland service centre from where
camels ferried goods in all directions. In an
area to the north-west of the town, known as
'Afghan town', it was not uncommon to see
400 camels.

Old Andado Station on the western edge of the Simpson Desert is a living museum of how the bush was pioneered. This thatched shed, along with split rail fences, windmills and the homestead itself give visitors a real taste of the hardship the early pastoralists endured. Once a thriving cattle station, Old Andado now offers camping facilities for passing travellers and houses the National Pioneer Women's Hall of Fame, which opened on Mother's Day in 1993.

The rustic kitchen of Old Andado Station. Built in 1922, the corrugated iron shack still had an earth floor when the legendary Molly Clark took up the lease for Andado with her husband Mac in 1955. Although Old Andado survives these days as a tourist attraction, Molly has plans to re-introduce cattle. The nearby Mac Clark Acacia Peuce Reserve, named after Molly's late husband, protects an isolated stand of these rare trees which are remnants of an ice age.

Concentric rings of spinifex in the Simpson Desert. Each season the grass dies off, dropping its seeds around the perimeter of the plant. With the first rains of the season, the seeds germinate and the new growth encircles the dying plant. Each successive season sees the ring increasing in diameter, until fire finally breaks the cycle.

The rising moon casts an eerie glow over the red dunes of the Simpson Desert, on Old Andado Station.

Overleaf: In a riot of colour, the sun sets on the multi-hued sandstone cliffs of Rainbow Valley, 100 kilometres south of Alice Springs in the Northern Territory. In previous times, this region had distinct wet and dry seasons. Wet season rains would soak deep into the sandstone, dissolving their red iron minerals. As evaporation 'pulled' water up during the dry season, the red minerals would also be drawn up, leaving the bleached, lighter coloured layers below.

The famous Alice Springs Camel Cup attracts cameleers from all over Australia, who pitch their skills against one another to control these recalcitrant animals and be first past the post. A favourite race of the day is the 'Honeymoon Cup', which sees the men who start the race attempting to stop their camels halfway around the track to collect their 'brides' for the day, before completing the course.

Camels were once important beasts of burden in the outback. However, the opening of the Ghan Railway to Alice Springs in 1929 heralded the beginning of the end of the camel's role as a transport animal. Many of the riders at the Camel Cup are direct descendants of the early cameleers. In more recent times the camels have assumed an important role in the tourist industry and many visitors to central Australia enjoy a safari aboard these 'ships of the desert'.

N O R T H E R N   E X P O S U R E

▶ Nature operates on a grand scale in the north of the continent. In the wet season violent tropical storms lash the country, lightning forks the sky, roads and rivers flood and cyclones tear at rooftops. During the dry the land bakes under a searing sun, the distance shimmers in a heat haze and ill-prepared travellers perish. The animals there seem larger-than-life as well, as are the stories about them.

▶ Probably the best known and most feared animal of the north is the saltwater crocodile (Crocodylus porosus). Growing to about 5 metres in length, 'salties' are well adapted to living in salt or fresh water and swimming holes far inland must be checked at the end of the wet to make sure that none of these dangerous beasts have taken up residence during the wet season floods. Although their diet consists principally of fish, saltwater crocodiles take large animals given the opportunity and have been responsible for numerous human deaths. The famous 'death roll' of this well adapted killer involves clamping its powerful jaws around the prey, then rolling underwater until its unfortunate victim drowns.

▶ Perhaps the most legendary of Australia's crocs was 'Sweetheart', whose name was coined from the area in which he lived, a billabong beneath Sweet's Lookout on the Finniss River in the Northern Territory. A wily old beast of enormous proportions, Sweetheart was 5.1 metres in length and weighed in at 780 kilos. In spite of living in an area frequented by crocodile shooters, Sweetheart was one of the few large crocs to have survived the intense period of hunting which took place in the 1950s and 1960s. But Sweetheart had a vendetta against outboard motors which was eventually to cost him his life. The reason he was so annoyed by them is unclear, but by the time the number of his attacks on boats had reached ten, people were beginning to cry for blood, particularly those who had been tipped out of their boats and lost valuable fishing gear in their ordeal. With crocodiles protected by this time, the Northern Territory's Conservation Commission set about trying to capture Sweetheart with a view to keeping him in captivity. But the canny old beast hadn't eluded hunters for 20 years to be captured now. After several months of intensive effort, using various types of baits and nets, Sweetheart was finally caught in July 1979, using a dingo as bait. Sadly, as the tranquilised Sweetheart was being towed across the river to a waiting vehicle, the towline snagged, his head was dragged under and water filled his lungs. Sweetheart died. One British newspaper carried the story that the 300-year-old, 136-stone (864 kilogram) crocodile's stomach contents had included 'crunched human bones and two motor boat engines'! In fact, Sweetheart's stomach contents were fairly typical of any large croc and included the remains of wild pigs, catfish, barramundi and two long-necked river turtles. Sweetheart never actually made an attack on a human being, in spite of plenty of opportunity to do so. His fury was always directed toward outboards and even though numerous people found themselves in the water with the huge croc after such an attack, he never made an attempt to harm them. These days the legend of Sweetheart lives on in the Darwin Museum, where his huge, scaly body is available for all to marvel.

▶ Among the staple foods of the crocodile are the barramundi which inhabit the waterways of the north. Legendary amongst anglers for their fighting ability and superb eating qualities, barramundi attract thousands of anglers to the north each year. 'Barra' are hermaphroditic. Until they reach a length of about 50 centimetres, which they do at approximately 6 years of age, all barramundi are males. They then change into their female form, which they retain for the rest of their life. To ensure that the breeding stock is maintained, anglers are required to release any fish under 55 centimetres in the Northern Territory. Even that is a big fish, but they do grow much, much larger. The biggest barra on record* was hooked in the Ross River in Queensland in 1977 and weighed in at a massive 21.32 kilos. Barramundi are found in both fresh and estuarine waters, though the estuarine variety are considered the prime target for the table. Even so, we were very pleased when we landed our first barra at Gregory National Park. A freshwater specimen weighing in at 5 kilos it tasted heavenly to us, baked on the coals under a star-lit sky. There followed some estuarine specimens and there is no doubt they are finer eating, but by the same token you can't beat your first-ever barra!

▶ Almost 2000 thousand kilometres away from the Gulf rivers of the north is another fish which draws anglers from far and wide. The fish is tailor and the location is Queensland's beautiful Fraser Island. Few would dispute that barramundi is a better table fish, but tailor offers excellent sport fishing on some of the most beautiful beaches in Australia. During the winter months tailor begin their run along the Queensland coast, congregating in great numbers along the seaward side of Fraser Island to spawn in early spring. It makes quite a sight as the anglers wade knee-deep into the surf, standing almost shoulder-to-shoulder as they cast into the gutters in which the tailor are feeding. It is also at this time of the year that the area is visited by humpback whales. On the way from their breeding grounds on the Great Barrier Reef to their summer feeding grounds in the Antarctic, the whales stop at Hervey Bay, between the mainland and Fraser Island, for one or two days rest.

▶ Fraser Island has become legendary in its own right, quite aside from its tailor fishing and visiting humpback whales. One hundred and twenty-five kilometres long and 25 kilometres wide, Fraser's 184,000 hectares make it the largest sand island in the world. Fringed by wide beaches, it has more than 40 perched, freshwater lakes nestled amongst the dunes of its interior. Their tannin-coloured waters are alive with turtles, brumbies are often seen drinking on their shores and gnarled paperbarks line their banks. Sand mining and logging were the major industries on the island until a long campaign by environmentalists saw much of the island protected during the 1970s. These days logging continues under strict controls, and Fraser is jointly managed by the Queensland National Parks Service and the Queensland Forest Service.

▶ Known as one of the three 'islands of wrecks', along with Kangaroo Island in South Australia and King Island in Bass Straight, Fraser owes its name to shipwreck victim Eliza Fraser. In 1836 Eliza was sailing from Sydney to Singapore with her husband James, Captain of the Stirling Castle, when the 351-tonne brig struck a reef off Rockhampton. The heavily pregnant Eliza took to sea in a pinnace along with her husband and nine other survivors. Whilst still at sea Eliza gave birth but the baby didn't survive. Without food or water, the men threatened to throw the Captain overboard if he didn't land on Fraser Island. Landing about 30 kilometres south of Sandy Cape, the men deserted and Eliza claims that her husband was speared by Aborigines, who took her captive. Eventually rescued by a convict who received a pardon for his bravery, Eliza returned to London, marrying the skipper of the vessel in which she travelled. In a tent in Hyde Park Eliza told a more lurid tale about the events surrounding her capture and captivity. It is reported that she charged sixpence admission to those wishing to hear the sordid details of her ordeal. Eliza Fraser died in an asylum.

▶ Today, Fraser Island's most famous wreck is the ss Maheno, a trans-Tasman luxury liner which was being towed to Japan for scrap in the winter of 1935 when an unseasonal cyclone struck. The towlines snapped and she ran aground. During WWI the ss Maheno was a hospital ship, but she was put to a rather different use in WWII when the RAAF used her for bombing practice. These days the Maheno is an important landmark on the island's east coast and a favourite spot for anglers who catch dart and tailor in the lee of her rusting hulk.

* ANSA record (Australian National Sportfishing Association)

Left: A billabong in Arnhem Land early in the dry season. By the end of the 'dry', water lilies have withered and died as the billabongs contract to a series of muddy pools.

Right: Early in the dry season, morning dew tips the grass stems with liquid crystal. The lush greens of the wet season are soon scorched to shades of brown and the waters in the billabongs are shallow and warm.

Previous page: This magnificent mauve lily bursts into flower after the northern wet season, when the billabongs are once again filled with water. The bulbs of these water plants are a favoured food of the Aboriginal people.

Overleaf: A legacy of dry season burning, the blackened trunks of swamp paperbarks contrast with the vibrant greens of the grasses around this billabong on the Gulf Track.

Left: The didgeridoo was adopted into the Aboriginal culture through contact with Indonesian traders in the seventeenth century. The instrument was originally made from bamboo, but these days it is usually made from a termite-hollowed eucalypt branch, preferably from the stringybark, woollybutt, ironwood or river red gum. The bark is stripped off and the instrument is often decorated with ochre and clay designs using totemic symbols. Sometimes the interior walls of the didgeridoo are thinned slightly at the ends, but no other modifications are made.

Right and Far Right: The rock art of the Aboriginal people depicts both dreamtime stories and episodes from everyday life. The paintings are executed in various pigments, including ochre which was traded widely between groups from various regions. The figures in the top left painting are the first Mirriwung men, the Gangi Nganang of Keep River National Park. The other paintings are in a cave in the Gulf region.

Overleaf: An Aboriginal cave littered with human bones and prolifically adorned with art, in the Gulf region of the Northern Territory. This cave features extensive examples of hand stencils in red ochre, including many made by young children.

In the harsh desert climate, the soft sandstone of the Lost City formations has weathered to create strange and wonderful shapes.

Previous pages: Located on McArthur River Station near Cape Crawford in the Northern Territory, the towering columns of the Lost City rise abruptly from the surrounding plain.

The white trunk of a ghost gum stands in stark contrast to the rich red termite mounds of Morstone Station in western Queensland.

Overleaf: A feature of the Australian outback, termite mounds vary in colour, size and shape, reflecting the soil colour and type of termite.

Left: The first light of the new day paints the walls of Lawn Hill Gorge, while a thin veil of mist evaporates from the surface of the cool water. An oasis in arid western Queensland, Lawn Hill is located adjacent to the famous Riversleigh fossil deposits.

Right: Overhanging figs have dropped their ripe fruit into this billabong in Lawn Hill Gorge National Park. When the figs are over-ripe and begin to ferment and rot, parrots literally fall out of the trees after gorging themselves on the fruit.

Overleaf: Majestic paperbarks line the edge of O'Shannassy River on Riversleigh Station in western Queensland.

The pinnacled towers of the karst cliffs of Chillagoe, in northern Queensland, had their origins as coral reefs and calcareous mud deposited 400 million years ago and subsequently uplifted. Heavy wet season rains have since furrowed the limestone to produce spectacular formations.

The setting sun paints the clouds with its palette of red-gold hues in a classic Gulf sunset at Karumba. Situated at the mouth of the Norman River, Karumba is the centre for the prawning industry of the Gulf of Carpentaria and is also an important centre for barramundi fishing in the Gulf rivers. At one time the town was a stopover point for the Empire Flying Boat Service which ran from Sydney to England.

Left: The industrious diggings of a sand crab pattern the shores of Chilli Beach on the east coast of the Cape York Peninsula. Fringed by swaying coconut palms, the beach is a true tropical paradise.

Right: A new moon rises against the backdrop of a vibrant sunset at Weipa. Located on the western coast of Cape York Peninsula, Weipa is the site of the world's largest bauxite mine.

Below: The receding tide textures the sand with graphic patterns.

The sun sets over the Endeavour River at Cooktown, in Queensland's far north. It was here that Captain James Cook beached his ship, *Endeavour*, in 1770 after it had been badly damaged on the Great Barrier Reef. More than 100 years later, gold was discovered in the nearby Palmer River, and Cooktown was finally on the map. By 1874 the town boasted a population of 30,000, serviced by 94 pubs, 30 brothels and a busy port. Once the gold was exhausted the population declined steadily and now stands at around 1600, many of whom are involved in the town's thriving tourism industry.

●Backed by the mountains of the Atherton Tableland, a crop of sugar cane awaits harvest near Cairns. The annual burning of the cane is almost a thing of the past now that cutting, stripping and mulching techniques are more widely practised. Consequently, the blackened face of the cane cutter, smoke heavy skies and the spectacular sunsets they produce are images of an era which is almost at an end.

●*Overleaf:* A view to Gloucester Island from the mango-growing centre of Bowen on the central Queensland coast.

●*Pages 168-169:* Each year thousands of anglers flood to Fraser Island for the annual tailor run.

Left: In the rainforest of Central Station on Fraser Island, vines use their host tree to climb upward in their quest for light.

Right: Its base splayed to support its massive bulk, this fig plays host to a variety of mosses and lichens which thrive in the warm, moist environment of the subtropical rainforest.

Previous pages: The wreck of the ss *Maheno* is a mecca for anglers on Fraser Island, who catch dart and tailor in the lee of her rusting hulk. Originally a trans-Tasman luxury liner, the *Maheno* was being towed to Japan for scrap when an unseasonal cyclone struck, snapping the towline and running the ship aground. Used as a hospital ship during WWI, she was put to rather different use in WWII when RAAF bombers used her for target practice.

Overleaf: Spectacular coloured sands are a feature of Fraser Island. Sand mining was once a huge industry on the island, but a long campaign by conservationists resulted in large areas of the island coming under protection by the end of the 1970s.

Page 175: A strangler fig entwines its host tree near Central Station.

Pages 176-177: The sun's dying rays tint a lone sea cloud with hues of pink and magenta.

BENEATH THE SOUTHERN CROSS

It's a big country all right! After 18 months of travel, covering 55,000 kilometres, we've only just scratched the surface. But the red dust of the outback is under our skin now and we'll be back there again and again. We set out to feel the solitude of Australia's remote and out-of-the-way places, to photograph its wild and desolate beauty and to meet the people who shaped this country.

We met many wonderful people on our journey; some whose crops had been decimated by rain yet were optimistic about a better season next year, others who'd spent days battling bush fires to save their stock and land. The resilience and bravery of these unsung heroes in the face of adversity was an inspiration.

There are others whom we didn't meet, but who are the stuff of tomorrow's legends. Mandawuy Yunupingu, lead singer of Yothu Yindi and named 1993 Australian of the Year, uses his music to send a message to the world about his people. Sarah Henderson of Bullo River Station became Australian Business Woman of the Year in 1991 and showed that guts and determination can overcome enormous obstacles. And there's Fred Hollows and his colleagues who with their trachoma programme did brilliant work amongst the Aborigines. Sadly, Fred died in 1993 but his work and his legend live on.

We didn't set out to tell the tales of all who pioneered the bush, but to give just a taste of some of the legends, myths and characters which shaped Australia. Our hope is that you have enjoyed this journey 'Beneath the Southern Cross'.

THANKYOU

Many people deserve our special thanks for their help and expertise in publishing this book:
Anne Esposito, the graphic artist, whose fax ran hot weeks on end as she worked her magic on the design
Helen Crasswill for editorial assistance,
Tim from True Colour copies who worked long hours to produce the colour photocopies for our layouts,
and to our friends and relatives who provided encouragement along the way.

PHOTOGRAPHIC INFORMATION

PHOTOGRAPHIC EQUIPMENT

With few exceptions the images in this book were photographed on medium and large formats using the Mamiya RZ67, the Art Panorama 6x17cm and the Linhof Master Technica 5x4". The 35mm images were shot on the Canon EOS 1.
The Art Panorama camera, fitted with a 90mm Nikkor f4.5 lens has an angle of view of 100°, which is well suited to the sweeping vistas of the outback. The 6x17cm image which it produces offers very fine detail when enlarged.

The Linhof Master Technica is a folding baseboard style camera which accepts 5x4" sheet film. The movements of the lens panel and the film plane enable the Scheimpflug principle to be employed, which renders all points of the image in sharp focus.
The Mamiya RZ67 offers the high resolution of a medium format camera with the versatility and accessories not available in larger formats. Lenses from 65mm to 180mm were used.

The range of lenses and portability of the Canon EOS 1 made it the camera of choice for wildlife and aerial shots. The lenses utilised ranged from 20mm to 600mm. Scarcely an image in this book was taken without the use of a tripod. For most 35mm and medium format work a Manfrotto ART055 with ball head was used; for 35mm work requiring the 300mm and 600mm lenses the Benbo was used, while the Linhof Technica was supported on a Gitzo.

Filters were used occasionally to improve the quality of the images. A polarising filter controlled reflected light thereby improving colour saturation; a graduated filter was used when required to control the sky; an 81C warm filter was used in heavy shade to compensate for the blue nature of the light.

The moody effect of some shots was achieved by extended exposures of up to 15 minutes. The star trace on the cover was a five hour exposure, f5.6, 200ISO. L&P Photographics are suppliers of all the equipment listed, which they complement with unparalleled technical advice, service and back-up.

FILM

The colour images appearing in this publication were shot exclusively on Fuji professional transparency film. The rich colour saturation and high resolution of Velvia made it our film of choice for landscape work. Where a higher film speed was required Fujichrome 100D was used. In the case of aerial work this was push processed to yield an effective film speed of 200 ISO, yet the film still retained excellent saturation and colour balance.

PROCESSING

Films were despatched from all parts of Australia to Bond Colour Laboratories in Melbourne. The professional staff at Bond ensured that our 'trannies' were processed to the highest standard and on their way back to us the very next day!

MURAL PRINTS

Limited edition mural prints of many of the images in this book are available. Printed by Bond, these stunning enlargements are offered in editions of 50 and can be purchased framed or unframed from Lightstorm Photography Pty Ltd ph (044) 466 007.

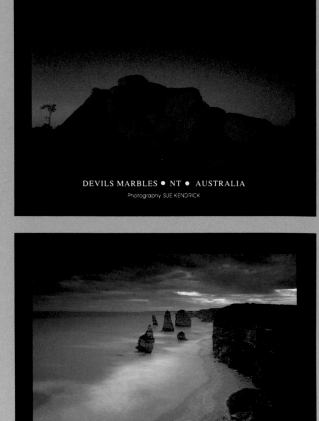

DEVILS MARBLES ● NT ● AUSTRALIA
Photography SUE KENDRICK

TWELVE APOSTLES●PT CAMPBELL NATIONAL PARK●VICTORIA●AUSTRALIA
Photography SUE KENDRICK

STRZELECKI DESERT ● SOUTH AUSTRALIA
Photography SUE KENDRICK

AUSTRALIA BENEATH THE SOUTHERN CROSS
ULURU STAR TRACE
Photography SUE and BRIAN KENDRICK

RIVERSLEIGH • QUEENSLAND • AUSTRALIA
Photography BRIAN KENDRICK

THE OLGAS • ULURU NATIONAL PARK • NT • AUSTRALIA
Photography SUE KENDRICK

YELLOW WATERS • KAKADU • NT • AUSTRALIA
Photography BRIAN KENDRICK

A U S T R A L I A
BENEATH THE SOUTHERN CROSS

Enjoy the grandeur and diversity of this vast continent by selecting from this superb series of posters.........

From the famous landmarks of Uluru and the Twelve Apostles to the remote red dunes of the Strzelecki Desert, Sue and Brian Kendrick travelled 55,000 kms to bring you this magnificent collection. Join in their journey by selecting from these beautiful reproductions, which are printed on quality art paper. Available framed or unframed, these prints will make a stunning addition to your home or office.

The images printed here, along with many others from the book, are also available as limited edition photographic prints. For more information please ph (044) 466007. To take advantage of our free poster offer, 'Uluru Star Trace', remove the cover sticker, attach in the space provided and include with a copy of the order form.

Post to: *Lightstorm Photography Pty Ltd P.O. Box 1167 Nowra NSW 2541 Australia Phone orders: (044) 466007 Fax Orders: (044) 466008*

QTY	DESCRIPTION		CODE	PRICE	TOTAL
	ULURU STAR TRACE	960mm x 500mm	001	Free with book purchase*	
	ULURU STAR TRACE	960mm x 500mm	001	24.95	
	RIVERSLEIGH	960mm x 500mm	002	24.95	
	OLGAS	960mm x 500mm	003	24.95	
	YELLOW WATERS	960mm x 500mm	004	24.95	
	DEVILS MARBLES	800mm x 600mm	005	24.95	
	TWELVE APOSTLES	800mm x 600mm	006	24.95	
	STRZELECKI DESERT	800mm x 600mm	007	24.95	
	FRAMING IF REQ: ☐ BLACK ☐ SILVER			50.00	

Plus Postage: **Australia** $5 Unframed **Oversees** $10 per order
$10 Framed Poster/s only

I enclose my cheque/money order made payable to: TOTAL $
Lightstorm Photography Pty Ltd
or debit my ☐ VISA ☐ MASTERCARD ☐ BANKCARD ☐ AMEX

Card No: ☐☐☐☐☐☐☐☐☐☐☐☐☐☐☐☐ Expiry date: ___ /

GUARANTEE If you are not satisfied with your purchase please return the order in good condition within 14 days and your full purchase price will be refunded.

▶ Please use a photocopy of this page when placing your order

Name: _____
Address: _____
_____ Postcode: _____
Ph: _____ Fax: _____
Signature: _____

After copying this order form attach cover sticker here as proof of book purchase and enclose postage as above

Carefully remove the cover sticker and place here for your
FREE
Uluru Star Trace Poster